{ CITIESCAPE }

MUMBAI*

{ CITIESCAPE }

JOE BINDLOSS

CONTENTS*

{ VITAL STATS 7. PEOPLE 9. ANATOMY 11. PERSONALITY 13. }

TRENDSETTER 17.
HISTORIC 31.
GLITZY 51.
ANIMATED 69.

GOLD STAR 91. PERFECT DAY IN MUMBAI 92.

VITAL STATS*

{ **NAME** Mumbai **AKA** Bombay; Bollywood; Bom }
DATE OF BIRTH Indian Bombay AD 500;
British Bombay 1661, when the few fishing villages
and the harbour were acquired by the British
HEIGHT 11m **SIZE** 440 sq km **ADDRESS** India
POPULATION 12 million to 15 million,
no-one is sure!

PEOPLE*

{ ***MUMBAI IS WELL ON THE WAY TO BECOMING THE WORLD'S MOST POPULOUS CITY.** Some experts predict that the population could top the 20 million mark within the decade. This crushing weight of humanity puts an incredible strain on the city and its resources. }

AROUND 60% of residents live in slums and the average wage is just 100 rupees per day – as some Mumbaikers earn million-dollar salaries, the average worker's wage may be even lower. However, much of this poverty is screened from view in Mumbai. Travellers tend to move in the same circles as middle-class Mumbaikers – a world of restaurants, coffee shops, mobile phones and shopping.

DESPITE THE SOARING population, the average Mumbai family has just two or three children – most of the population increase comes from people moving into Mumbai from other parts of India.

ANATOMY*

{ *MUMBAI IS SEPARATED FROM THE MAINLAND BY THE ULHAS RIVER, BUT }
MOST OF THE CITY is built on reclaimed land, so it feels more like a peninsula than
an island. Colaba, a rapidly developing village, is at the southernmost end of the spit.
The old colonial quarter, Fort, is immediately north of Colaba, and the main business
district is further west at Nariman Point. From there, the elegant sweep of Marine Drive
runs north to famous Chowpatty Beach. The posh shopping districts are in north Mumbai,
while Mumbai's infamous slums are concentrated around polluted Mahim Creek.

THE BEST WAY to get around Mumbai is by taxi or commuter train – suburban rail
services fan out across the city. Long-haul trains leave from Victoria Terminus and
Mumbai Central Station, and hundreds of flights land daily at the airports in Sahar.
Mumbai's crazy urban sprawl is concentrated in the south – the far north of Mumbai
island is preserved as Sanjay Gandhi National Park.

11.

PERSONALITY*

{ *MANY PEOPLE WONDER WHY MUMBAI ISN'T THE CAPITAL OF INDIA. It's the home of the Indian stock exchange and the financial hub of the nation, so this executive-type city has everything going for it. Mumbai leads the country in music, fashion and film, courtesy of the huge Bollywood film industry, and the population is half as big again as the next-largest Indian city. Maybe this massive scale is what scares off the politicians. Running a nation as large as India is hard enough from a well-organised city like New Delhi – in a runaway metropolis like Mumbai, it might well be impossible. }

THE WORLD'S third-largest city, Mumbai is a continuous, heaving mass of humanity. With all these people, you might expect it to be maddening, hectic, overpowering… but for the most part it's quite the opposite. This is India's most tourist-friendly city, and as long as you avoid the morning and evening rush hours the atmosphere is surprisingly calm, even at popular tourist places like Chowpatty Beach.

13.

HOWEVER, THERE'S A WORLD of difference between calm and boring – Mumbaikers have energy by the kilowatt and a contagious sense of enthusiasm that sweeps you along. Nowhere is this expressed more vividly than in Mumbai's movie-houses. The mark of a good film is durability – it's not uncommon for Mumbaikers to see the same film 10 or 15 times as a sign of appreciation. The wealth generated by Bollywood and the financial institutions of Fort and Nariman Point has fuelled the creation of a new urban elite. Middle-class neighbourhoods like Bandra, Breach Candy and Juhu Beach offer a window onto a new India – post-industrialised, self-confident and rapidly catching up with Europe and America. This is exactly the kind of India that foreign economies are afraid of, full of educated, highly skilled workers who know exactly how much their time is worth.

PREDICTABLY, the money flowing around Mumbai is very unevenly distributed, but those who have it enjoy an international lifestyle of fast food, impulse shopping and mobile phones. Nevertheless, the city has a palpable sense of history – of course all the Raj-era buildings are a constant reminder. The streets of the old British quarter are lined with fading 18th-century banking houses, covered in insane numbers of columns and statues.

THE THING PEOPLE notice most about Mumbai is the sense of movement and animation. There's always something going on somewhere in the city and it doesn't have to be loud and crowded to be memorable – though it often is.

LIVELY, GLAMOROUS yet sedate: peek into the photo album of Mumbai's fascinating life over the chapters that follow.

14.

TREND SETTER*

{ ***IT'S THE FASHION AND FILM CAPITAL OF INDIA, SO MUMBAI DOESN'T FOLLOW TRENDS, IT SETS THEM.** The films produced in Bollywood are seen by nearly a sixth of the world's population, giving Mumbai incredible power over the Indian fashion scene. If an outfit appears on a catwalk it gets seen by a few fashionistas; if it appears in a Bollywood blockbuster it sets the style for the nation, much to the chagrin of many Indian traditionalists. }

BOLLYWOOD HAS a long history of pushing the boundaries of Indian society. When the first screen kiss was aired in 1978 it caused riots across the country. When a lesbian relationship was shown onscreen in the 1997 film *Fire*, cinemas across India went up in flames. More recently, Shyam Benegal stirred up a storm with his biopic *Netaji Subhas Chandra Bose*, which suggested that the Independence hero secretly married a non-Indian. Some commentators insist that Bollywood is the main force driving the moral decline of Indian civilisation.

17.

{ ALL OF THIS is water off a duck's back to the young, urban elite of Bandra and Breach Candy. Young people in Mumbai are itching to embrace the 21st century. Jeans and T-shirts are fast replacing the traditional salwar kameez and 40% of Mumbaikers now own mobile phones, with the largest uptake among 15- to 24-year-olds. In fact, mobile phones are probably driving the biggest social change of all – young people dating without their parents' consent. }

IF YOU ARE young and rich in Mumbai, life is a non-stop parade of novelty ring tones, air-kisses and parties. The bars in Bandra and Juhu Beach are swooningly sophisticated, with glitzy cocktails, sequin-soaked outfits, star-studded guest lists and pulsing Bollywood anthems.

NOT ALL SIGNS of globalisation bring as much disapproval from the city's moral guardians. Fast food has taken Mumbai by storm, and for every McDonalds there's a branch of Cream Centre, Copper Chimney or Bombay Blue serving Indian favourites fast-food-style, complete with treats for kids and super-sized cokes. Espresso coffee is another growing Mumbai obsession – chain coffee shops are opening up on every street corner, bringing a few nervous glances from the India Tea Board. For travellers this all provides a reassuring sense of home. Mumbai is arguably the most tourist-friendly city in India and growing numbers of travellers are coming here just for the shopping and nightlife.

LIKE THE SLICK, kaleidoscopic and crazy Hindi movies the city churns out with machine-gun rapidity, it's a city that on the face of it makes little sense but is still enormous fun. However, some long-term visitors mourn the decline of Mumbai's uniquely Indian character. Fashions may come and go but one thing seems permanent in Mumbai – the inevitable march of progress.

MUMBAI MASTI*

{ *MASTI, OR FUN, IS THE UNOFFICIAL SOUNDTRACK TO MUMBAI.** The word crops up in a thousand Hindi movie soundtracks, evoking a lifestyle of luxury, wealth and celebrity. With the dramatic expansion of the Internet, there are now hundreds of masti websites devoted to the stars, songs and movies of Bollywood. The concept of masti preoccupies Mumbai's middle class. For young urbanites, masti means dressing provocatively, partying with friends, drinking, dancing, dating – most of the things that teenagers in the West take for granted. It's a lifestyle which is presented in a thousand Bollywood films, but it's often harder to achieve in real life. }

INDIANS HAVE recognised the healing power of laughter for centuries and laughing as a group exercise is believed to cure everything from mood swings to long-term depression. More than 70 laughter yoga clubs meet at parks and beaches across Mumbai every morning for a therapeutic giggle. They must be doing something right, as laughter clubs have now started up in more than 40 countries – laughter is even being used for corporate stress management!

21.

STAGS OF STYLE*

{ }

* IT WASN'T LONG AGO THAT THE ONLY CLUBS IN MUMBAI WERE STUFFY RELICS OF THE RAJ, reserved for aristocrats, politicians and industrialists. Luckily, people power has reclaimed clubbing from the port and cigar set. Modern Mumbai has lounge bars and nightclubs that could hold their own in any of Europe's clubbing capitals, complete with whirling lights, postmodern décor and ear-trembling sound systems.

THE CITY HAS BECOME an established stop on the international DJ circuit, but there's no shortage of local talent, and the sounds of sitar and tabla are liberally mixed in with the trance and techno beats. Almost all the clubs set aside at least one night of the week for Bollywood soundtracks. However, there is one problem for Mumbai clubbers – most clubs have a couples-only policy. Locals beat this proscription by partying in mixed groups or paying extra for the upmarket hotel nightclubs that admit stags – the local term for single men or women.

22.

CATWALK CAPITAL*

{ *** MUMBAI IS THE BEATING HEART OF THE INDIAN FASHION INDUSTRY, AND THE FASHION HOUSES HAVE A STEADY SUPPLY OF GORGEOUS MODELS** to wear their latest creations, courtesy of Bollywood. Sponsored by the beauty chain Lakmé, Mumbai's Fashion Week is the biggest event in the Indian fashion calendar, showcasing local designers like Tarun Tahiliani, Krishna Mehta, Ashish Soni and Narendra Kumar. Exuberant design, vivid colours and container-loads of sequins make Indian fashions stand out in a crowd. }

WHY BUY CLOTHES off the peg when they can be made to measure by Mumbai's leading designers for the same price as high-street fashions in Europe and America? Gentlemen need look no further than the upmarket tailors on Veer Nariman Road, while ladies have the pick of the exclusive designer fashion houses in Bandra and Breach Candy. For ready-made fashions straight from the design studios, there are the boutiques in Colaba and the ultra-modern Phoenix Mills shopping centre.

25.

BEAUTIFUL BOM*

{ * **JUST AS YOU MIGHT EXPECT FROM THE HOME OF INDIAN FASHION, MUMBAI RESIDENTS LIKE TO LOOK THEIR BEST.** The city is packed with beauty parlours and luxury spas offering everything from botox jabs to reflexology. }

MANY OF THE luxurious pamperings are based on traditional Indian Ayurvedic medicine. Herbs from the foothills of the Himalaya and blossoms from the jungles of South India are pounded into skin creams, massage oils, face-packs and wraps, and smeared all over the rich and beautiful in opulent spas across the city. Many more people relax in Jacuzzis or steam rooms or pamper themselves with an oil massage and facial at a full-service hotel spa.

FEW MUMBAI MEN have the time or inclination for this level of self-indulgence. The most popular act of male grooming is the great Indian shave, available from barbershops across the city – a perilously close shave with a straight razor, followed by moisturiser, aftershave, a face massage and an alum rub.

26.

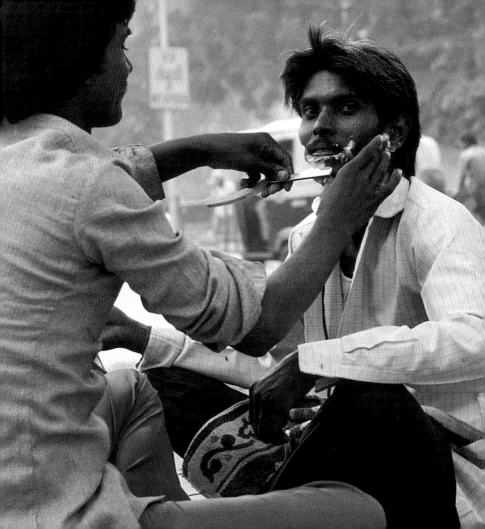

A NEW MUMBAI?*

{ *THE FLOODS OF THE 2005 MONSOON ONLY REINFORCED THE IDEA THAT MUMBAI IS DROWNING UNDER THE WEIGHT OF ITS OWN POPULATION. Plans are now afoot for the creation of a brand new skyscraper city on the north side of Mahim Creek. Tourists may be drawn to Mumbai by the crumbling Raj-era monuments, but the city financiers want to attract foreign investors, not tourists. If the plan takes off, Mumbai will be transformed into a financial powerhouse, the focal point of the first South Asian tiger economy. }

NOT EVERYONE is happy about the proposals, however. More than 90,000 slum tenements have already been bulldozed to make space for new construction, leaving 300,000 homeless. The plans have also alarmed environmentalists. The Mahim Creek acts as a filter for the incoming Arabian Sea and as a drain for the polluted Mithi River. Scientists have long warned about the folly of allowing construction to disturb these natural drainage patterns.

29.

HISTORIC*

{ * **HISTORY IN MUMBAI HAS BEEN FORGED BY A SUCCESSION OF EMPIRES.** The }
seven islands that make up the city were first taken over by the British government in
1665 and leased to the East India Company. The area, then called Bombay, developed
as a trading post and soon became the trading headquarters for the whole west coast
of India.

MANY LOCALS still remember the fight against British colonial rule. Older Mumbaikers
have seen their city transformed from occupied territory into the leading economic light
of a new, free India. Many stages in the struggle for Independence were acted out on
these streets – Mahatma Gandhi coordinated the Independence movement from a
small apartment in Breach Candy and the Quit India campaign was launched in the
park on August Kranti Marg.

PROBABLY THE MOST lasting legacy of the British occupation – aside from tea and
the English language – is Mumbai's magnificent colonial architecture. Buildings like the

Gateway of India and the Chhatrapati Shivaji Maharaj Museum are an incredible fusion of architectural styles, with Gothic arches, Germanic turrets, Gujarati balconies and Mughal domes. By today's standards it all looks incredibly ostentatious, but in its time this was the height of sophistication.

BRITISH-ERA buildings are covered in statues representing Britannia, Industry and Commerce – neatly sidestepping the fact that the Indians did the industry and the British got the commerce. With Mumbai's plans to become an economic powerhouse, the next generation of skyscrapers could well feature statues of British businesses being overtaken by Indian ingenuity.

MANY CUSTOMS OF the Raj still persist despite the relentless march of modernisation. Cricket remains a national obsession and the sound of leather on willow can still be heard all over Mumbai, particularly on warm afternoons at the Oval Maidan. English high tea is another Mumbai institution, served by waiters in starched white uniforms at a handful of fading colonial teahouses. However, the soaring popularity of the cappuccino may send this custom the way of the dodo.

MANY LOCALS WOULD be more than happy to forget Mumbai's colonial past, but for visitors, the fading relics of the Raj are an essential part of the city's charm. On the day that Victoria Terminus is torn down to make space for a shimmering modern train station, a part of Mumbai will die forever – fortunately for travellers there's no serious chance of this happening in the near future.

FOR NOW, tourists can walk along wide boulevards lined with 19th-century British banks and peek into forgotten churches with extravagant memorials to the soldiers and generals who forged the British Empire. Considering the suffering caused and the lessons learned since Independence, it's a rather humbling experience.

GRAND
CENTRAL STATION*

{ *** MUMBAI IS AWASH WITH EXTRAVAGANT RAJ-ERA ARCHITECTURE, BUT WITH-OUT DOUBT THE CITY'S** finest colonial monument is Victoria Terminus. Described by Jan Morris as 'the central building of the whole British Empire', Mumbai's surreal central station is a cross between St Peter's in Rome and the Taj Mahal in Agra, with hints of a tiered wedding cake thrown in for good measure. The whole building is covered with gargoyles, arches, statues, stained glass, buttresses and domes, none of which seem to serve any practical purpose. }

A STAGGERING 2.5 million commuters pass through the station every day, but few pause to look up at the glorious vaulted ceilings covered in carvings of lions, peacocks, and monkeys swinging through jungle trees. The only problem is finding a place to stop and appreciate these details – if you stand still, the crowds will sweep you along and onto a commuter train to the suburbs in a flash.

35.

PLACE OF CAVES*

{ * **ELEPHANTA ISLAND, 10 KILOMETRES BY SEA FROM THE GATEWAY OF INDIA, IS MUMBAI'S MOST FAMOUS HISTORICAL TREASURE**. Carved into the naked bedrock of the island are a series of stone temples dating back to the 5th century AD, when the island was known as Gharapuri, or Place of Caves. }

THE TEMPLES of Elephanta are dedicated to Shiva Mahadeva, who's usually depicted with three heads, representing the three sides of his character – creator, preserver and destroyer. The central statue in the main cave temple shows Mahadeva in all his glory, six metres high and covered in ritual finery. The scenes of moving statues in Ray Harryhausen's 1970s *Sinbad the Sailor* films were almost certainly inspired by these temple carvings.

REGARDED BY MANY as the finest piece of sculptural expression in India, the complex covers 6500 square metres, with numerous antechambers hewn from the solid rock. Even the detailed and delicate figures on the walls were created by carefully chipping away tiny pieces of stone.

37.

COLABA SEAFRONT *

{ * **NOWHERE CAPTURES THE HISTORY AND CHARACTER OF OLD MUMBAI QUITE LIKE THE COLABA SEAFRONT.** Hundreds of pivotal moments in the city's history have occurred here over the centuries, not least the final departure of the British at the end of colonial rule. The waterfront is dominated by the elegant Taj Mahal Palace and Tower, Mumbai's finest Raj-era hotel, built by an outraged Parsi industrialist who was banned from Mumbai's British-owned hotels for being 'a native'. Satisfyingly, it's the only colonial-era hotel still in business. }

ACROSS FROM THE TAJ is the Gateway of India, built in 1924 to demonstrate the durability of British rule – shortly before Gandhi and Nehru brought the colonial administration crashing to its knees. It's probably the definitive symbol of the city and dozens of photographers loiter in front of the monument offering souvenir snaps to the hordes of Indian tourists who descend on Colaba every morning.

38.

BOWLING 'EM OVER*

{ * **AS THE BIRTHPLACE OF CRICKET SUPERSTAR SACHIN TENDULKAR, MUMBAI HAS CRICKET IN ITS BLOOD.** When international cricketers come to town, they play at the Wankhede Stadium on Marine Drive. But Mumbaikers stage their own energetic one-dayers on the Oval Maidan, a large section of parkland in front of Mumbai University. There's no better way to spend a sunny afternoon than relaxing on the Maidan and joining in the shouts of 'Howzat!' as another wicket falls. }

MANY OF MUMBAI'S most impressive Victorian buildings, like the ornate High Court, were constructed on the edge of the Oval Maidan during the building boom of the 1860s and '70s, when the Maidan formed a leafy promenade along Bombay's seafront. Mumbai University, one of Mumbai's true architectural gems, recently celebrated its 125th birthday. The centrepiece of the Gothic- and Mughal-inspired university buildings is the 95-metre-high Rajabai Tower, which resembles a church tower crossed with a minaret and topped by a Hindu shikhara (temple tower).

CRICKET IS more than India's favourite sport – it's a matter of national pride, particularly when India plays against Pakistan. During the test cricket season the world's finest cricketers slog it out at the Wankhede Stadium, while nearby in the streets children mimic their every move with tennis balls, planks of wood and broken packing cases for stumps. Generations of Mumbaikers have bowled their first overs and hit their first sixes on the Oval Maidan by Mumbai University.

PICTURE PALACES*

{ *MUMBAI HAS A GROWING COLLECTION OF MODERN MULTIPLEXES, BUT BY FAR THE MOST ATMOSPHERIC PLACES** to see the latest Bollywood blockbusters are the Art Deco movie houses from the final days of the Raj. The elegant Regal on Colaba Causeway was Bombay's first Art Deco cinema, opening in 1933. Designed by Charles Stevens, it was also the first cinema in India with air-conditioning. The Dalai Lama saw his first film here in the 1960s as a young exile from Tibet. }

OTHER MUSEUM PIECES include the rocket-shaped Eros Cinema by Churchgate Station, which was the first major building construction on the reclaimed land in Back Bay. The quietly fading Art Deco Metro on MG Road was opened in 1938 as a vehicle for showing MGM's movies, but quickly shifted to locally made productions. The ground on which the cinema stands is still officially leased for 999 years at a rent of one rupee per year.

HIGH TEA*

{ }

* AS THE FORMER CAPITAL OF THE BRITISH RAJ, MUMBAI HAS INHERITED PLENTY OF VENUES FOR AN OLD-FASHIONED POT OF ENGLISH TEA. Of course, the tea is actually Indian, grown on the well-watered slopes of Darjeeling and Assam.

PROBABLY THE MOST charming spot for high tea is the Tea Centre, tucked beneath the offices of the India Tea Board on Veer Nariman Road. It's fittingly colonial in style, with heavy wooden furniture, monumental pillars, Victorian glass lamps and a pianist playing 1930s show-tunes in the corner. The tea comes in burnished silver pots, served by waiters in starched turbans and cummerbunds.

INDIAN CHAI – sweet tea with milk and spices – is Mumbai's favourite drink though, and is served by street vendors everywhere. It faces growing competition, however, from espresso coffee. Coffee bars are opening all over the city, serving cappuccinos, caffe lattes, espressos and all manner of frozen concoctions topped with whipped cream and sprinkles to Mumbai's growing economic elite.

49.

GLITZY*

{ *FOR MANY IN INDIA, MUMBAI IS THE MOST GLAMOROUS PLACE ON THE }
PLANET. This is the cutting room of Indian fashion, the birthplace of Indian cricket and the heart of the Indian stock exchange. Think of it as New York for Americans or London for the British and you'll have some idea where Mumbai stands in the national psyche. There are a thousand rags-to-riches stories about hopeful young men and women from the countryside who came to Mumbai and made it big, and just as many stories of people who vanished forever into Mumbai's sprawling slums.

ABOVE ALL, MUMBAI is the home of Indian cinema. Centred on Bollywood in north Mumbai, the Indian film industry is the biggest on the planet, producing an amazing 1000 films every year – around twice the number of films that come out of America, its closest competitor. The very first Indian feature – *Raja Harishchandra* by Dadasaheb Phalke – was filmed here back in 1913, and from these humble beginnings Indian cinema exploded into a multibillion dollar industry.

LIKE LOS ANGELES, the city is packed with aspiring actors and actresses hoping for their big break. And as you might expect, there are more wannabes than success stories. Those who make it, however, can look forward to a life of extravagant luxury, assuming of course that they don't get caught out in a financial or moral scandal – a fate befalling a growing number of Bollywood superstars.

MOST VISITORS ARE happy to just watch the stars on screen or catch a passing glimpse of their favourite celebs in bars and clubs around Mumbai. Currently, the most popular Bollywood nightspots are up in Juhu Beach, but the stars are as fickle as cats and places go in and out of fashion at the drop of a hat pin.

DRESSING LIKE THE stars is a different story. The styles on screen quickly make it onto the racks in Mumbai boutiques, and you can get dazzling, spangly outfits made to measure by Mumbai designers that will stand out like a tiger on rollerskates on the streets of Europe or America. The snazziest screen outfits are reserved for the dance routines in all-singing, all-dancing masala movies – even the jewellery that appears in these blockbusters soon shows up in upmarket Mumbai jewellery shops.

STUDIOS ARE OFTEN looking for extras for background scenes, and although volunteers are strenuously discouraged (most film studios are closed to anyone without an appointment), many visitors to the city have been 'spotted' and asked to play a small role in a Bollywood smash. Scouts are usually sent to Colaba, often around the Gateway of India, to conscript European-looking extras. You could get lucky and end up as canon fodder in a gory dramatisation of the Indian Uprising, or you could spend a boring day loitering on a hot set for a five-second appearance in the background of a street scene.

MOVIE MANIA*

{ *THE OPENING NIGHT OF A BOLLYWOOD BLOCKBUSTER IS A FILM FESTIVAL IN
MINIATURE, particularly if the movie stars Shah Rukh Khan, Amitabh Bachchan or
Preity Zinta. Crowds queue around the block at most Mumbai cinemas, and the city
bubbles with gossip about the stars and their personal lives.

IF A FILM is a hit, people dance in the aisles and the soundtrack goes straight to the
top of the pop charts – the action smash *Sholay* ran for five consecutive years. If it's a
flop, audiences desert the cinemas in droves.

SERIOUS SCREEN FANS used to take the experience one step further and do exclusive
Bollywood tours, with demonstrations from stuntmen and dance choreographers, talks
from directors and visits to working studios to see the stars in action. However,
increased security fears have currently put tours on hold, so getting beyond the gates
into the Town of Magic is near impossible unless you are recruited as an extra. }

55.

BOLLYWOOD GIVES Mumbai incredible control over the nation's tastes and mores. The songs, stars, fashions and moral codes of Mumbai are flashed up daily on the biggest billboard in the world, the screens of India's 13,000 cinemas. Bollywood does occasionally sound a wrong note – Shah Rukh Kahn's rapping in *Kal Ho Naa Ho* singularly failed to start off an Indian hip-hop revolution – but for the most part, what Bollywood says goes.

REACH FOR THE STARS *

{ *SEEING THE STARS OF BOLLYWOOD ON THE SILVER SCREEN JUST ISN'T ENOUGH FOR SOME PEOPLE.** Social climbers and movie wannabes frequent Mumbai's trendiest bars and restaurants looking for a chance to brush up against Rani Mukerji or Aishwarya Ray. }

MOST OF MUMBAI'S red-carpet bars are north of the centre in Bandra, Pali Hill, Juhu and Lower Parel – all are full of Bollywood beauties, disco divas, sports stars, city yuppies and catwalk queens. The Bollywood gossip magazines buzz with tales of who was seen in which bar drinking with whom. However, partying with the party people doesn't come cheap. Drinks cost more than many Mumbaikers earn in a week and only the most glamorous patrons make it past the bouncers on the doors.

59.

LIFE'S A BEACH*

{ *ANY FAN OF BOLLYWOOD MOVIES WILL ALREADY KNOW THAT CHOWPATTY
BEACH IS THE MOST ROMANTIC LOCATION IN MUMBAI. Bollywood superstars
have wooed their leading ladies on the golden sands, and every evening thousands of
couples recreate the scenes with romantic promenades along the shoreline. Not everyone's happy about this, though: the municipal authority even installed giant spotlights
on the beach to prevent couples using the darkness for illicit liaisons. }

STILL, AFTER DARK a carnival atmosphere prevails and the beach comes alive with
fairground rides and stalls selling ice-cream, gola (crushed ice with fruit syrup) and
bhelpuri (spicy Mumbai salad). This is also where the riotous climax of the Ganesh
Chaturthi festival takes place: millions of people descend on the beach to submerge
the giant statues of the elephant-headed deity.

BY DAY, teenagers sunbathe and swim – fully clothed of course – at the south end of
the beach, while local Koli fishermen haul up their nets at the base of Malabar Hill.

61.

SEA AND BE SEEN *

{ *** BRONZED BODIES, GOLDEN SANDS, LIFEGUARDS. NO, WE'RE NOT TALKING ABOUT BAYWATCH.** Juhu Beach is where the wealthy and the fashionable come to unwind and frolic by the Arabian Sea. Juhu had its heyday in the 1970s but it's still a very upmarket locale, full of huge international beach resorts, coffee shops, beauty parlours and – for some reason – authentic Italian bistros. Somehow, the scene on the beach is more appealing than the idea of swimming in the water – it's filthy. But the festive atmosphere on the shore is captivating and kids, along with eco-friendly adults, will be thrilled by the human-powered fairground rides. }

FURTHER SOUTH, sweeping along the shore of Back Bay towards Chowpatty Beach, is Mumbai's favourite promenade, Marine Drive. Every day from first light the residents of the drive's million-dollar Art Deco apartments walk along the strip to see and be seen. Young couples and their chaperones come for the romance – at night, the parade is lit up by thousands of lights, earning it the nickname 'The Queen's Necklace'.

SEQUIN CITY*

{ * **THE IDEA FOR THE SEQUIN PROBABLY CAME FROM CHINESE PLATE ARMOUR, BUT INDIA HAS CLAIMED THIS GLITZY ORNAMENT AS ITS OWN,** the perfect adornment for a country that prides itself on making magic out of the commonplace. So shoes and belts come encrusted with sequins, saris are embellished with glittering rainbow cascades and evening bags flash and bedazzle... disco divas are in sequin heaven. The upmarket shoe shops and fashion boutiques of Bandra and Colaba offer some amazing creations that almost collapse under the weight of their sparkles and spangles. And of course, sequins play a major role in Bollywood spectaculars – how else to depict the glittering headdress of a Hindu god? }

INDIAN COMPANIES BEGAN manufacturing sequined trimmings for the overseas market in 1945, catching the eye of a Western public embracing flamboyance for the first time since World War II. Never before had the glitter of gold (albeit gold-coloured plastic) been so available to the masses.

64.

MALL FEVER*

{ *SHOPPING MALLS ARE THE LATEST FAD GRIPPING MUMBAI.** Leading the pack is the Phoenix Mills shopping centre in Lower Parel, a former cotton mill reborn from the flames as a cutting-edge mall with bars, restaurants, fast-food chains and retail outlets for all the big Mumbai fashion designers. There are even boutiques here that turn into bars once the sun goes down. The biggest downtown shopping mall is Crossroads in Breach Candy; it's full of top-of-the-range international designer label shops and fast-food joints. }

SHOPPING TOURISM is another fad luring visitors to the city, and it isn't just about clothes – perfumes, electronics, jewellery, DVDs and antiques all cost less in Mumbai, and the range of goods on offer is fast catching up with Hong Kong or Singapore. Different districts have their own specialities – glamour girls fight through the crowds on Linking Road in Bandra for perfumes, shoes and fashions; backstreet boys browse the brand-name emporiums on Colaba Causeway for the latest offerings from Nike and Tommy Hilfiger.

ANIMATED*

{ *PART OF THE APPEAL OF A HUGE, INSANELY CROWDED CITY LIKE MUMBAI IS ITS SHEER HUMAN ENERGY.** A big city is something that gets into the blood. Once you've lived somewhere heaving like Shanghai, Sao Paolo, Bangkok or Mumbai, smaller cities seem curiously quiet... even a little spooky. Based on the population within the designated city limits, Mumbai is now the third-largest city in the world, well ahead of London and New York and five times larger than Paris or Rome. }

EVEN MORE REMARKABLE is the fact that Mumbai's estimated 12-million-plus residents are squeezed into an area one third the size of Sydney. Around 30,000 people live on every square kilometre of turf and 60% of the population is crammed into the high-rise slums of central Mumbai. This all puts an incredible strain on the city's infrastructure. Mumbai's commuter trains are a sight to behold, with hundreds of passengers hanging from every doorway.

DESPITE THE CROWDS, Mumbai doesn't feel unduly desperate or impoverished. Mumbaikers are stoic about their predicament and optimistic about the future. One inevitable side effect of living in a city with this many people is resilience. Locals seem able to bounce back from any calamity – and they've had their share in recent years, including the dramatic floods of 2005 which inundated half the city.

THE MOST INTERESTING places to be in Mumbai are exactly those places where thousands of people get together. The annual Ganesh Chaturthi festival attracts nearly 10 million devotees and the streets are filled with fireworks, music, singing and dancing, and of course those famous neon-pink statues of Ganesh. If you miss this once-a-year spectacular, the Sassoon Docks and the Mahalaxmi dhobi ghats (the outdoor laundry) provide a similar sense of excitement on a smaller scale, year-round.

THE GLITZY SCENE in Bollywood and Bandra is a world away from the experience of most Mumbaikers. To get a feel for how ordinary people live, chat to students in the bars on Colaba Causeway, spend a day at the Mahalaxmi races or join the swirling evening crowds on Chowpatty Beach doing what Mumbaikers enjoy most – munching bhelpuri. Bhelpuri is Mumbai's favourite snack, but don't expect lettuce and tomatoes and a drizzle of balsamic. It's a tongue-twisting mix of chickpea-flour noodles, puffed rice, green mango, coriander, onion, potato, peanuts, chilli and sweet tamarind chutney.

A DAY
AT THE RACES*

{ *** MUMBAIKERS LOVE TO GAMBLE AND THE BEST RETURNS BY FAR ARE OFFERED BY THE HORSE RACES AT THE MAHALAXMI RACECOURSE.** From August to April the city is gripped by racing fever and the public stands at the racecourse explode with wild cheers and bitter cries of disappointment as punters egg on their favourite racers and riders. }

BETTING IS BIG business in Mumbai – massive amounts of rupees are made and lost on every race, and mobile phones are confiscated at the gate to stop spectators cheating the odds at downtown betting shops.

THE BIGGEST EVENT on the racing calendar is the Indian Derby in February – it's Mumbai's fashion day on the field and everyone dresses up, with all the customary outsized hats. The best place to be is the members' terrace, but winners celebrate in style in the swish Gallops Bar looking right out over the turf – the menu runs to victory cigars and champagne on ice.

72.

FISHING FRENZY*

{ *FROM WELL BEFORE DAWN, THOUSANDS OF KOLI FISHERWOMEN GATHER TO }
RECEIVE THE DAY'S CATCH at the Sassoon Docks, the largest fishing quay in Mumbai.
The atmosphere is frenetic as tonnes of fish and seafood are thrown from basket to
basket along the quayside to the ice houses at the back of the waterfront. Most of the
fish is spirited away to restaurants and hotels by waiting porters, but the fisherwomen
keep some aside to sell at local markets, supplementing the small income they make
from mending nets, hauling and drying fish and shelling prawns.

DESPITE THE MUCKY work, many of the workers wear brilliantly coloured traditional
costume, bedecked with mirrored panels and dangling braids. This is one of the few
places in Mumbai where traditional Koli costume can still be seen.

JUST BEWARE – by mid-morning, the sun starts to bake the dead shrimps on the
quayside and the reek of fish rises to blanket the whole of south Colaba.

BEFORE THE BRITISH came to Mumbai, it was the home of the Koli, a fishing tribe that plied the coast of Maharashtra as far back as the 2nd century BC. Although they're now massively outnumbered by migrants from other parts of India, the Koli still dominate the local fish trade. The Sassoon Docks are the landing point for most of the fish and prawns that end up on tables in Mumbai's restaurants, and are without doubt the noisiest, busiest and most overwhelming part of Mumbai.

THOUGH THE KOLI community is best known for its distinctive dress, Koli people also have their own language, food and deities. The name 'Mumbai' is derived from Mumbadevi, the patron goddess of the Koli tribes.

LIVING LAUNDRY*

{ *WASHING MIGHT SEEM AN UNLIKELY ATTRACTION, BUT THE HUGE DHOBI
GHATS AROUND MAHALAXMI TRAIN STATION ARE A FASCINATING SPECTACLE. }

Every day, from dawn until sunset, more than 5000 dhobi-wallahs pound, push and
pummel the city's washing in giant concrete troughs. Looking down onto the dhobi
ghats from Mahalaxmi train station, there is laundry as far as the eye can see, and row
upon row of open-air concrete wash pens, each fitted with its own flogging stone. Even
the laundry from Mumbai's upmarket hotels ends up down there somewhere among
the water tanks and dripping sheets.

THE CLOTHES ARE first soaked in sudsy water and thrashed on the flogging stones,
then tossed into huge vats of boiling starch and hung out to dry. Stubborn stains are
removed by soaking garments in a boiling vat of caustic soda. Drying takes place
on long, brightly coloured clotheslines and heavy wood-burning irons are used for
pressing. Once they're ironed, the clothes are piled into neat bundles to be returned to
their owners.

78.

THE MAHALAXMI dhobi ghats have been the workplace of Mumbai's traditional launderers for generations. Unimaginable numbers of shirts, saris and underpants pass through the washing pens every day, some for the hundredth or even thousandth time – it's the world's largest outdoor laundry. Miraculously, few items of clothing ever go missing in this soapy human maelstrom. Launderers keep track of every item using a secret system of 'dhobi marks', which are invisible to the untrained eye. This laundry accounting system is so accurate that police have been able to track down criminals using just the dhobi marks on clothing found at crime scenes.

BIZARRE BAZAARS*

{ *** MUMBAI'S PUBLIC MARKETS AND DENSE BAZAARS BUZZ WITH ENERGY, PARTICULARLY DURING THE ALPHONSO MANGO SEASON,** when the softest, sweetest mangos in the world are sold in their thousands. Perhaps the quirkiest market is the Chor Bazaar, or 'thieves' market', centred on Mutton Street – occasional gems of Victoriana turn up among the broken record players and 1970s bric-a-brac. **}**

TOURISTS HAGGLE for 'I Love Mumbai' T-shirts and fake divers' helmets in bustling Colaba Street Market, just north of the Sassoon Docks. Locals prefer the heaving passageways of Crawford Market, Mumbai's largest and the last outpost of British Bombay. Its Norman-Gothic exterior is graced by bas-reliefs designed by Rudyard Kipling's father, Lockwood Kipling. Inside, the market is crammed with wholesalers selling dried nuts, bulk fruit, imported candy, haberdashery, wigs and other household essentials. At the back is the harrowing 'wet market' where Mumbai butchers ply their trade. Be warned: Mumbaikers are not squeamish about where their meat comes from. Some of the joints of lamb here have eyes…

83.

RIDING THE RAILS*

{ *** THE FIRST TRAIN ON INDIAN SOIL RAN IN BOMBAY BETWEEN BORI BUNDER AND THANE ON 16 APRIL 1853.** Even more auspicious was the year of 1891, when toilets were introduced in first class. The first electric train ran on 3 February 1925 between Bombay VT and Kurla – so you can see train travel is in Mumbai's blood. }

IN MODERN MUMBAI around six million people ride the commuter trains into the centre of the city daily, flooding from the northern suburbs to the central stations to work in the office towers of Fort, Colaba and Nariman Point. The morning and evening rush hours see incredible crowds surge onto every train, leaving half the passengers dangling from the doorways – according to the Mumbai rail authority, up to 5000 people cram onto every train, but there are only seats and standing room for 1500. This dramatic oversubscription puts a huge strain on the system, and it's a major safety issue, but somehow the trains keep running, and are usually on time.

84.

GANESH CHATURTHI*

{ * **IT SEEMS APPROPRIATE THAT THE PATRON DEITY OF CROWDED MUMBAI IS ELEPHANT-HEADED GANESH,** the god of wisdom and prosperity and the remover of obstacles. Hindus from across Maharashtra descend on Mumbai in late August or early September for the huge Ganesh Chaturthi festival celebrating the birthday of the much-loved god. They fill every hotel and swell the already huge crowds in the streets. }

EACH YEAR more than 9000 gaudy statues of Ganesh are displayed around Mumbai and paraded through the streets, before being ceremonially thrown into the sea at Chowpatty Beach, Juhu Beach and various other spots around the city. Some statues stand more than 10 metres tall and have to be hoisted into the ocean with giant cranes.

THE CROWDS ARE BIBLICAL – or should that be Vedic? – in scale and the atmosphere is electric. Unfortunately, the often-overlooked side effect of the festival is the massive increase in water pollution from the tonnes of plaster, mud and toxic paint used to make the giant idols.

87.

HINDU MYTHOLOGY HAS several stories about Ganesh. According to one legend, Parvati, goddess of love, gave birth to Ganesh and raised him in her husband Shiva's absence. One day, as Ganesh stood guard while Parvati bathed, Shiva returned and asked to be let in. Ganesh staunchly refused. Shiva, enraged, lopped off the boy's head, only to later discover with horror that he had slaughtered his own son. He vowed to replace Ganesh's head with that of the first creature he came across, and that's how Ganesh came to have an elephant's head.

90.

GOLD STAR

MUMBAI GETS A GOLD
STAR FOR ITS LIMITLESS
ENTHUSIASM. MUMBAIKERS
LAUNCH THEMSELVES INTO
EVERY NEW FASHION AND
ACTIVITY WITH INCREDIBLE
GUSTO, BUT ALWAYS WITH A
UNIQUELY INDIAN POINT OF VIEW.
IT'S THE PERFECT ATTITUDE
FOR A CITY THAT SETS THE
NATION'S TRENDS.

MY PERFECT DAY

JOE BINDLOSS

{ * The perfect Mumbai day starts with a street-side cup of chai and a leg-stretching stroll along the Colaba Seafront to catch the ferry to Elephanta Island. If you get up early, you can have the temples to yourself and be back in Colaba for coffee and a muffin long before the hordes arrive. Next, stroll north to Fort to soak up the fading Raj ambiance of Mumbai University and the Oval Maidan and do a spot of shopping in the state emporiums on Dr DN Road. For lunch, take your pick of the Mangalorean seafood restaurants for a spicy fish curry. In the afternoon, set aside a few hours to admire the Mughal miniatures and Maratha weapons in the Chhatrapati Shivaji Maharaj Museum then jump in a taxi to Chowpatty Beach to watch the sun go down with a plate of bhelpuri. For supper, there's only one choice – Khyber, an Aladdin's cave of Northwest Frontier cuisine on Mahatma Gandhi Road. For evening drinks, Leopold Cafe in Colaba is an old favourite, or head to one of the swish bars on Waterfield Road in Bandra for a Mumbai Sling (like a Singapore Sling but with ginger and coriander).

}

JOE HAS WRITTEN FOR MORE THAN 25 GUIDEBOOKS FOR LONELY PLANET, INCLUDING SEVERAL EDITIONS OF LONELY PLANET'S *INDIA* GUIDE AND THE *BEST OF* GUIDE TO MUMBAI. He first came to India as a backpacker in the early 1990s and something hit a note – since then, he's been back nearly a dozen times, lured by the food, the energy and the incredible range of landscapes and experiences. There's something about India that keeps Joe coming back for more. When not researching guidebooks, Joe lives in northeast London with his partner Linda, and a growing collection of Indian musical instruments, Buddhist statues and Tantric masks.

PHOTO
CREDITS

{

PAGE 43 Playing cricket at the Oval Maidan
Christophe Bluntzer/Impact Photos

PAGE 44-5 Young boys ready to bat at Shivaji Park
Catherine Karnow/APL/Corbis

PAGE 46 The Art Deco Regal Cinema in Colaba
Greg Elms/Lonely Planet Images

PAGE 48 Orange pekoe tea and scones set out on a tray at the Tea Centre
Mick Elmore/Lonely Planet Images

PAGE 50 A model displays hand-crafted diamond bridal jewelery at a fashion preview
Punit Paranjpe/Reuters/Corbis

PAGE 53 The Intercontinental Hotel
Jon Arnold Images/Alamy

PAGE 54 A Bollywood studio
Jon Arnold Images/Alamy

PAGE 56-7 An Indian artist paints a Bollywood film poster at a workshop in Mumbai
Punit Paranjpe/Reuters/Picture Media

PAGE 58 Fans reach out to Bollywood actress Preity Zinta at the Apsara Film Producers Guild awards
Arko Datta/Reuters/Picture Media

PAGE 60 Children play at Chowpatty Beach at sunset
Alain Evrard/Impact

PAGE 63 Couples enjoy the cool early morning air along Marine Drive, Nariman Point
Karen Trist/Lonely Planet Images

PAGE 65 Shoes for sale at a stall on Colaba Causeway
Mick Elmore/Lonely Planet Images

PAGE 66 The Nirmal Lifestyles Mulund shopping mall
Dinodia Images/Alamy

PAGE 68 The big wheel at Chowpatty Beach is man-powered
Mark Henley/Panos Pictures

PAGE 71 Commuters and travellers in chaotic motion at a railway station
Ladi Kirn/Alamy

PAGE 73 Keeping an eye on the horse at Mahalaxmi Race Course
Joerg Boethling/Still Pictures

PAGE 74 Koli fisherwomen carry loads of fish on their heads
Dinodia Images/Alamy

PAGE 76-7 Koli fishermen tend their nets
Ladi Kirn/Alamy

PAGE 79 Traditional laundrymen (dhobis) wash clothes in open laundries known as dhobi ghats
Arko Datta/Reuters/Picture Media

PAGE 80-1 Clothes drying at a dhobi ghat
Homer Sykes/Impact Photos

PAGE 82 A market stall attendant takes a rest
John Sproule/Alamy

PAGE 85 Crowed commuter trains
Chris Stowers/Panos Pictures

PAGE 86 A large statue of Hindu god Ganesh is ready to be immersed in the sea at Girgaum Chowpatty
Dinodia Images/Alamy

PAGE 88-9 Indian women prepare for Sun worship at the annual festival of Chhatha Pooja
Dinodia Images/Alamy

CITIESCAPE

MUMBAI

OCTOBER 2006

**PUBLISHED BY LONELY PLANET
PUBLICATIONS PTY LTD**
ABN 36 005 607 983
90 Maribyrnong St, Footscray,
Victoria 3011, Australia
www.lonelyplanet.com

Printed through Colorcraft Ltd, Hong Kong.
Printed in China.

PHOTOGRAPHS
Many of the images in this book are available
for licensing from Lonely Planet Images.
www.lonelyplanetimages.com

ISBN 1 74104 937 7

© Lonely Planet 2006
© photographers as indicated 2006

LONELY PLANET OFFICES
AUSTRALIA Locked Bag 1, Footscray, Victoria 3011
Telephone 03 8379 8000 Fax 03 8379 8111
Email talk2us@lonelyplanet.com.au

USA 150 Linden St, Oakland, CA 94607
Telephone 510 893 8555 TOLL FREE 800 275 8555
Fax 510 893 8572 Email info@lonelyplanet.com

UK 72–82 Rosebery Ave, London EC1R 4RW
Telephone 020 7841 9000 Fax 020 7841 9001
Email go@lonelyplanet.co.uk

Publisher ROZ HOPKINS
Commissioning Editor ELLIE COBB
Editors JOCELYN HAREWOOD, VANESSA BATTERSBY
Design MARK ADAMS
Layout Designer INDRA KILFOYLE
Image Researcher PEPI BLUCK
Pre-press Production GERARD WALKER
Project Managers ANNELIES MERTENS, ADAM MCCROW
Publishing Planning Manager JO VRACA
Print Production Manager GRAHAM IMESON